The
Hea...
Neolithic
Orkney

Mini Guide
by Charles Tait

1st Edition

ISBN978-1-909036-12-3

The Heart of Neolithic Orkney Mini Guide
1st Edition
Published by Charles Tait
Kelton, St Ola, Orkney KW15 1TR
Tel 01856 873738 Fax 01856 875313
charles.tait@zetnet.co.uk   charles-tait.co.uk

This book is dedicated to my grandfather,
Charles William Tait (1885-1967),
who introduced me to the Maeshowe winter sunset

ISBN 978-1-909036-12-3

The Heart of Neolithic Orkney
Mini Guide
by Charles Tait

CONTENTS

1st Edition

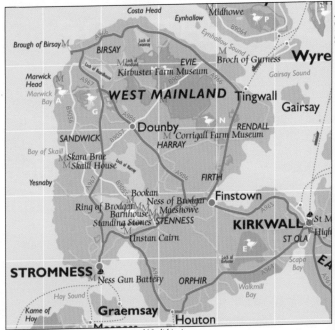

The West Mainland, showing the principal Neolithic sites

NEOLITHIC ORKNEY The term "Neolithic" (Greek *neos*, new and *lithos*, stone) was coined by Sir John Lubbock in 1865. It covers the period from c.10000-2000BC during which agriculture, buildings, settlements, writing, weaving, pottery making and much else developed. From the first domesticated crops being grown in the Middle East around 10000BC to the oldest known house in Orkney is about 6,000 years.

Today Orkney retains a vast archaeological treasury of buildings, artefacts and evidence from this time. In recognition of this, "The Heart of Neolithic Orkney" was inscribed on the World Heritage List by UNESCO in 1999. Because of their outstanding universal value, "*The monuments of Orkney, dating back to 3000-2000BC, are outstanding testimony to the cultural achievements of the Neolithic peoples of northern Europe.*"

This guide covers all of the main monuments which are part of the nominated site, as well as many of the associated contemporary places of interest. The village of Skara Brae, stone circles of the Ring of Brodgar and the Standing Stones of Stenness and Maeshowe chambered cairn are described in depth.

The major settlements at Barnhouse and Ness of Brodgar both show that much remains to be discovered about Neolithic Orkney. Isolated standing stones, such as the Watchstone, chambered cairns, such as Unstan and more enigmatic sites, for example the Ring and Cairn of Bookan, are also included.

The Neolithic Timeline, opposite, sets the Orkney period in a European context. People first reached Orkney within about 4,000 years of the end of the last Ice Age. By 4000BC they were well settled here, farming livestock, growing crops, fishing and building comfortable dwellings. They also created elaborate houses for their dead, large stone circles and immense buildings which are only now coming to light.

The maps included here are sufficient to locate all of the places described, but the Ordnance Survey 1:50,000 sheet 6 (Orkney - Mainland) or the 1:25,000 sheet 463 (Orkney - West Mainland) are essential visitors' tools. *The Orkney Guide Book*, 4th edition, by the same author describes the whole archipelago in detail.

NEOLITHIC TIMELINE

BC

c.12000	End of last Ice Age
c.11000	Orkney separated from Scotland
c.10200	Start of the Neolithic period
	First crops Einkorn, Millet, Spelt
c.9000	First towns in Middle East
c.8000	First hunter-gatherers in Scotland
	Domestication of animals
c.5300	Vinca symbols in use, Serbia
c.5000	Wheat, Oats, Flax domesticated
c.4500	Neolithic Age in NW Europe
	Vinca and other symbols in use
c.3600	Knap of Howar oldest date
	Unstan Ware pottery
	Malta Temples
c.3300	Barnhouse oldest
	Ness of Brodgar oldest
c.3200	Stalled cairns appear
	Isbister oldest date
	Maeshowe tombs appear
	Skara Brae oldest date
	Ness of Brodgar earliest
	Writing invented Mesopotamia
c.3100	Knap of Howar latest
	Quanterness Cairn
	Grooved Ware pottery
c.3000	Standing Stones
	Quoyness Cairn
	Skara Brae phase II
	Wall of Brodgar, Ness of Brodgar
c.2800	Maeshowe built
c.2700	Ring of Brodgar built
c.2600	Ness of Brodgar structure 10
	Woodland virtually gone
c.2500	Cairns latest date
	Skara Brae latest
c.2300	Ness of Brodgar demolished
c.2200	Ness of Brodgar latest
c.2000	Start of Bronze Age in Orkney

The Knap of Howar is the oldest stone-built house in northwest Europe

NEOLITHIC AGE The similarities between tombs and artefacts from the North of Scotland and Orkney suggests that people arrived via Caithness. There were cultural links with the Highlands and Islands, Ireland and Wessex during the Neolithic Age. Farming was well established in Orkney over 6,000 years ago.

Houses One of the oldest standing houses in Western Europe, the Knap of Howar, is on the island of Papay and dates from about 3600BC. The buildings at Skara Brae in Sandwick, Rinyo on Rousay, Noltland on Westray, Pool on Sanday as well as Barnhouse and Ness of Brodgar in Stenness all date from slightly later, about 3100BC. These are established settlements, built by accomplished stonemasons and reflect the work of a settled people, rather than new arrivals.

Skara Brae hut 1

Skara Brae Street

The houses were quite sophisticated, being built with double-skinned drystone walls. Midden material was often packed between these walls and surrounded them on the outside. No similar stone houses remain in Britain, or indeed Europe, and their origin is obscure. However, the buildings at the Knap of Howar have two interesting features.

There is a strong resemblance in shape and internal features with some of the early chambered cairns, and the outline is distinctly boat-shaped. Later Neolithic houses, such as at Skara Brae, are much squarer, with built-in bed spaces, and resemble the Maeshowe-type chambered cairns. Elsewhere in Britain plentiful timber would have been available for construction; its lack in Orkney was made up for by the excellent building stone.

Since driftwood from North America was very likely available in quantity, they would have had wooden fittings, while whalebone may also have been used for rafters. Roofs quite probably used some of the boat-building tradition with

Knap of Howar doorway

High quality masonry work, Knap of Howar

woven Willow or Hazel supporting a covering of leather and turf, parts of old boats or even flagstone slates. Heather, reed or straw thatch may also have been used. Heather ropes were likely used to secure the structures. The only evidence of flagstone roofs so far is from the Ness of Brodgar. A brief survey of more recent

NEOLITHIC DOMESTIC SITES TO VISIT

Stenness	Barnhouse
	Ness of Brodgar
Sandwick	Skara Brae
Rousay	Rinyo
Wyre	Braes of Ha'Breck
Westray	Noltland links
Papay	Knap of Howar
Sanday	Pool
Eday	Green

THE FIRST SETTLERS

Skara Brae hut 1 is very well preserved and measures about 6m by 6m internally

ruined houses shows that roof coverings and timbers are the first to be salvaged. Thus the archaeological record is perhaps biased in favour of what was not salvaged after abandonment.

The houses may well have had wooden fittings and doors. Interior furniture only survives as stone beds, dressers, cupboards, stone-lined tanks and hearths. Wood, leather, textiles and bone would all have made the houses comfortable. The recent finding of painting at the Ness of Brodgar suggests that colour may also have been a feature.

Fuel could have been dried dung, seaweed, turf, driftwood or whalebone, but not much peat as this only started to develop much later. The houses had good,

lined, drains. At Skara Brae the houses are equipped with cells which were perhaps toilets, store rooms or pantries. In all cases the quality of the stone work is very impressive. It is easy to imagine the domestic life of the inhabitants.

These people had a good and stable standard of living, with time and energy to build elaborate monuments like Maeshowe, the Ring of Brodgar and the impressive buildings on the nearby Ness. Nothing is known of their language or culture, except that which can be gleaned from their buildings, artefacts and the landscape. Barley and some Wheat were grown, while cattle and sheep plus some pigs and goats were kept. Seabirds and fish were important in their diet and deer were hunted.

Boats To reach Orkney and the other Scottish islands, good boats, seamanship and a working knowledge of the dangerous waters was required. These vessels had to carry substantial numbers of people, animals, seedcorn, tools and other goods. They journeyed far down the coasts of Britain, and had done so since the end of the Ice Age.

Offshore fishing for large Cod and Ling was practised. None of this was possible without a good knowledge of the tides, skerries and weather patterns in these waters. Excellent hooks have been found in middens, fashioned from heated cartilage, which are extremely strong, yet flexible.

Their boats were probably built with a stout wooden frame, most likely with Oak timbers and a framework of Willow or Hazel. Although leather, perhaps tanned with Oak bark could have been used as a skin, this would have been heavy and easily damaged when wet. Much more likely is a woven fabric cov-

Skara Brae doorway with lining and jambs

ering made from Flax or Nettle fibres. Both are very resistant to rotting, immensely strong and easily grown in quantity. Finally the skin would have been tarred with copious amounts of pitch. Such boats would have been easy to construct and maintain as well as being light to haul out.

Skara Brae bed without the lining

Hand quern at Knap of Howar

THE FIRST SETTLERS

The large house at Barnhouse is 7m by 7m internally

Clothing The old idea was that the Skara Brae people wore undressed leather skins but this is highly unlikely. Hunter gatherers would have used light, protective and hard wearing materials to make their clothes. The Neolithic people had a wide range of options besides skins, including woven vegetable fibres, felted or woven wool as well as woven grass, nettle fibres or straw. Bone pins would have been used in place of clasps.

Food & Drink Remains of pots varied from tiny to over 60cm in diameter. Two different styles of pottery artefacts have been found in these Neolithic sites. Round flagstone pot lids are common. Saddle querns were in widespread use to grind the Wheat and Barley, though probably the latter was mostly eaten after malting which makes the grain much more digestible, as well as sweet to the taste. Large quantities of malt was also

A small Grooved Ware pot

Skara Brae bone pins

Excavation work in progress, Ness of Brodgar

used to make ale, which was preserved and flavoured with Meadowsweet, a very common Orkney wild flower.

There was plenty of milk, fish, sea birds as well as domestic beef and lamb. Many edible wild plants which are mostly ignored today would have been gathered to be used medicinally, as flavouring, as preservatives or as vegetables. Silverweed, Sea Plantain, Marsh Marigold,

Scurvygrass, Sorrel, Lyme Grass and Bullrush are all edible and locally common. Poisonous plants such as Henbane, which occurs in Orkney, may have been used as hallucinogens.

Seals were certainly exploited, perhaps more for their oil and very durable skins than their meat. Whales were much more plentiful and strandings would have been seen as a great bounty from the sea.

Well built wall and path at the Ness of Brodgar

Ness of Brodgar "neuk bed"

BURIAL OF THE DEAD

The interior of Maeshowe is monumental and incorporates standing stones

BURIAL OF THE DEAD was clearly taken very seriously, and at least in some cases, excarnation was practised. Bodies were left in the open for some time to allow the flesh to decay, and only some of the bones were placed in the tombs. Some osteological studies suggest that the people had short and unhealthy lives, but there is no evidence that this was universal.

The Neolithic people were able to construct these elaborate monuments for their dead as well as impressive stone circles and very large buildings such as at the Ness of Brodgar. This suggests that their society was prosperous and well-organised.

There are similarities between pottery and other artefacts found in Portugal, southern England, Ireland and Orkney, suggesting that there were contacts with people in these areas. Little is known about the boats of the time, but vessels able to transport people and their animals across the Pentland Firth or to fish offshore would have been more than adequate to undertake longer journeys as well.

Climate and climatic change may well have had a lot to do with early settlement. Analysis of pollen shows that by about 5900BC the land was covered with grassland, birch-hazel scrub and ferns. After the arrival of farming in about 4000BC this was replaced by more open vegetation , probably due to their grazing animals and clearing for cultivation. While there is no direct evidence of manuring, it is hard to believe that these people did not notice the beneficial effects of dung and seaweed on the land, especially given the evident importance of the midding to them.

The vegetation changes started about 3800BC, continued for some time, and by 2600BC there were few trees left. Recent tree-ring studies of old Irish Oaks suggest that there was a sudden deterioration of climate about 2350BC, which is about the time of the latest Neolithic dates. One theory is that a large comet or asteroid struck Earth at this time, causing a nine-year winter.

By 1300BC extensive peat bogs were developing, making much marginal land unworkable, and overwhelming remaining woodland. By this time the landscape would have been very similar to that of the early 20th century.

Cuween cairn near Finstown

CHAMBERED CAIRNS TO VISIT

This is only a selection of the most accessible and best-preserved cairns. Those marked in **bold** are covered in this book. Please see *The Orkney Guide Book 4t*[b] edition for full descriptions of all of the sites.

Bookan type

Sandwick	**Bookan**
Rousay	Taversoe Tuick
Eday	Huntersquoy

Orkney-Cromarty type

St Ola	Head of Work
Stenness	**Unstan**
Rousay	Blackhammar
	Taversoe Tuick
	Midhowe
	Knowe of Yarso
	Bigland Long
Westray	Cott
Eday	Braeside
Stronsay	Kelsburgh
S Ronaldsay	Tomb of the Eagles

Maeshowe-type

St Ola	Wideford Hill
Stenness	**Maeshowe**
Sandwick	**Ring of Bookan**
Firth	Cuween Hill
Egilsay	Onziebust
Papay Holm	Long Cairn
Sanday	Mount Maesry
	Quoyness
Eday	Vinquoy Hill

BURIAL OF THE DEAD

The Tomb of the Eagles at Isbister is also stalled, but has three side cells

Chambered Cairns are tombs which are characteristic of Neolithic times. They are stone-built and typically have a central chamber with an entry passage and sometimes one or more cells off the main chamber.

Knowe of Yarso is a small stalled cairn

Orkney has many of these houses for the dead, many of which are well preserved, and well-built. These tombs were built by the Neolithic farmers, the oldest date in Orkney being from about 3200BC, and many continued in use for up to 800 years before final sealing.

Although there is a range of sizes and design, there are basically two types: which have been dubbed the Orkney-Cromarty Group (OC) and the Maeshowe Group (MH). The former type is related to similar cairns in Caithness, while the latter is unique to Orkney. In many ways these tombs are similar to the contemporary houses at Skara Brae and Knap of Howar.

The OC type, of which there are about 60 in Orkney, is characterised by having upright stalls set into the side walls, shelves at one or both ends as well as sometimes along the sides and rounded corbelling for the roofs. Low-roofed cells occasionally lead off the main chamber. The pottery type found in these cairns was *Unstan Ware*. These are wide, round bottomed pots, which may or may not be decorated, and are also associated with the Knap of Howar in Papay, as well as Stonehall in Firth.

The MH type have rectangular chambers with high corbelled ceilings, and cells which may also have high roofs, but they lack the upright stalls of the OC type. They also tend to be built of larger stones, often massive and normally very well cut and fitted together. There are only 12 examples of these unique structures. Where pottery was present it was always *Grooved Ware*, flat-bottomed pots, quite distinct from the *Unstan type*. This association is also unique.

Unfortunately most sites were cleared out in the past without the benefit of modern techniques. However, several cairns were excavated recently and produced much data. The Maeshowe-type cairns at Quanterness (St Ola) and Howe (Stromness) and the Orkney-Cromarty type cairn at Isbister (South Ronaldsay) yielded many human and animal bones, artefacts and other material from which much has been deduced about the lives of the people buried there.

At Pierowall on Westray, a probable Maeshowe-type cairn was discovered during quarrying. This yielded an intricately carved stone, now in the Westray Heritage Centre. It has spiral markings very like the one found at Church on Eday, now in NMS. Similar designs at Newgrange in Ireland and elsewhere suggest cultural connections.

Upper floor of Taversoe Tuick chambered cairn on Rousay

BURIAL OF THE DEAD

Midhowe on Rousay is very large

Osteology The picture gained from studies of bones recovered at Quanterness and Isbister is of a hard life. Few people lived longer than 30 years, and most died before 25. Arthritis was common in adults, while mortality in childhood was high. Usage of the tombs lasted for several centuries. In these excavations, remains of large numbers of individuals were found, with partial

Stone work like "Unstan Ware" pottery

skeletons of up to 400 people at each of Isbister and Quanterness.

Some cairns, such as Maeshowe, contained no bones on excavation. Most earlier excavations failed to yield the detail of the recent work. The lack of bones and other artefacts in many instances may simply mean that the cairns were cleared out at some unknown time in the past, perhaps when they were decommissioned and finally sealed.

Some tombs appear to have had an association with animals, Sea Eagles at Isbister, dogs at Burray and Cuween and sheep, cattle or deer at others. Whether these, together with the many pot sherds also found, are the remains of funeral feasts or offerings to the dead is an open question. It is interesting to note that nicknames for people from particular parishes and islands are still in common use. Some of these may be ancient, and many are somewhat derogatory.

That the Neolithic people went to such lengths in housing their dead, in contrast to later times, suggests that ancestors were very important to them. While much has been discovered about the material aspects of these people's lives, little has been revealed about their rituals and social organisation. The very large effort implied in the construction of these monuments suggests that the society was well organised and had resources beyond mere subsistence farming.

The development progression of chambered cairns may have started with the apparently simple, and possibly early, Bookan type, through the various increasingly elaborate stalled cairns to the Maeshowe type. The last category is unique to Orkney and culminated in the eponymous impressive structure. Dating evidence is lacking for many sites.

Unstan cairn in Stenness

Skull from the Tomb of the Eagles

"Unstan Ware" pots - largest two from Unstan, the small bowl is from Taversoe Tuick

NMS

STANDING STONES

The Ring of Brodgar originally comprised 60 stones, of which 27 remain intact

STANDING STONES Apart from houses and chambered cairns, the Neolithic people also erected standing stones, stone circles and henges. These are some of the most impressive monuments from this time, especially the collection of megaliths between the Stenness and Harray Lochs.

The henges include the Ring of Brodgar, the Standing Stones of Stenness and the Ring of Bookan. Isolated standing stones include the Watchstone and those at Barnhouse, Deepdale and Hindatuin. The impressive rock cut ditches at the three henges represent a massive construction project. Selection, quarrying, transport and erection of the monoliths seems like very hard work in the absence of metal and power tools. The planning and laying out of the sites also required considerable expertise.

Many visitors, illustrious or not, have proposed reasons for the erection of these monuments. They have usually suggested rituals, which is archaeological shorthand for "don't know", and often divined all sorts of bizarre things. What is clear is that the Neolithic people were very much in tune with their environment which obviously included the cycles of the sun and the moon.

The sites selected for these monuments are not accidental. They are situated in the heart of the West Mainland amid a low lying landscape of farmland, moorland and water and surrounded by a bowl of hills. Although there may be slightly more farming activity now than in Neolithic times, these are timeless places.

Traditionally it has been assumed that an ancient quarry near Vestrafiold in Sandwick (HY239218) is the source of stone for the Standing Stones, Brodgar and Maeshowe. Several large stone slabs still lie where they were quarried, a number even still resting flat on small stones awaiting transport. The largest is over 5.5m long.

Recent geological examinations at Brodgar suggest that this is true for some, but perhaps not all of the stones. It has been suggested that several of the monoliths may have originated elsewhere in

Midsummer sunset at the Ring of Brodgar

STONE CIRCLES & HENGES TO VISIT

Stenness	Standing Stones
	Ring of Brodgar
Sandwick	Ring of Bookan

STANDING STONES TO VISIT

Stenness	Watchstone
	Barnhouse
	Odin Stone (site of)
	Comet Stone
Harray	Hindatuin Stone
Birsay	Quoybune
Stromness	Deepdale
Rousay	Yetnasteen
N Ronaldsay	Holland
Eday	Setter Stone
Shapinsay	Mor Stein

Low Moon at the Standing Stones of Stenness

Standing Stones

Summer sunset at the Standing Stones of Stenness, with the Loch of Stenness and the Hoy Hills in the ba

the West Mainland, from a number of quarries. They might have been delivered from different parishes as part of a grand community enterprise.

The Odin Stone was destroyed in 1814

Regardless of the reasons for and the logistics of their construction, the three henges represent a considerable design challenge for a time when it is claimed that there was no form of writing or notation. The circles are near perfect, the ditches symmetrically cut and the standing stones are accurately set. Whatever the source of the megaliths, they had to fit an overall concept. Powerful forces in Neolithic society drove the building of stone circles all over Britain and Northern Europe. The Orkney henges date from the early part of the 3rd millennium BC and are some of the oldest in the UK.

What archaeologists like to call rituals probably did involve the sun and moon, perhaps to decide on specific dates for festivals. The main activities were probably fertility rites including dancing, music, song, drinking, use of drugs and a good deal of sexual activity. These people were established farmers, accomplished fishermen and had at least occasional

connections with distant communities. But they also depended on the return of the sun, the fertility of the soil, the fecundity of their animals and crops and their own successful reproduction.

The Watchstone at midsummer

Midwinter sunrise at Stenness

The Barnhouse Stone in midwinter

ALIGNMENTS

Midwinter sunset at the Watchstone, where the sun "rolls" down the north side of the Ward Hill

ALIGNMENTS It is almost impossible to visit the Orkney Neolithic sites around the solstices without noticing obvious alignments to the rising and setting sun. The best known event is the afternoon midwinter sun illuminating the chamber of Maeshowe. Local people have long said that the Watchstone is a more significant observation position.

Sun The winter solstice was clearly an important event as it is marked from multiple places on several dates between early December and the end of January. Thus the precise date can be accurately known despite many cloudy days. Of particular interest are the "flashing events". The sun disappears behind a hill and then momentarily reappears on the other side, as for example in Stenness.

The movements of the Sun are reflected in alignments at Bookan, Brodgar, the Standing Stones, Barnhouse and also at the Ness of Brodgar. Things are complicated by the fact that an unknown number of standing stones and buildings have been felled or destroyed. In recent times

some monoliths have been re-erected. Others have been toppled by lightning strikes, careless farmers or infamous vandals.

Chambered Cairns nearly all have a day when the rising or setting sun shines through the passage. Perhaps this is of significance, as also may be the dates when the light of the rising or setting Moon enters. Both Wideford and Cuween are illuminated at the equinox, and the Tomb of the Eagles bathes in the May Day sunrise.

The destroyed cairn at Pierowall may well have had a southwest orientation, with its impressive lintel stone facing the sunset. Holm of Papa Westray South catches the rising sun in November and January.

Solar and Lunar Calendars Midwinter and midsummer are obvious set points in the calendar. A number of festivals seem to be very ancient. These include those now called St Brigit's (*Imbolc*, Old Irish *i mMbolg*, in the belly, pregnancy of ewes) on 1st February. May Day (*Beltane*, Celtic *Belo-tenia*, bright fire) was for long celebrated with bonfires on 1st May.

Lammas (OI *Lughnasa*, festival) was a fair held on 1st August or later, when people met to trade produce, make contracts and young people sought romance. Called Halloween today, *Samain*, (OI *Latha na Samna*, Festival Day) was a major festival celebrating the end of the harvest and the onset of winter on 1st November. Many of these dates were taken over by the Christians with varying degrees of success.

Detailed surveys of many Neolithic monuments have produced conflicting evidence for a calendar, thought by some to be the precursor of the so-called Celtic Calendar. Most likely many of the alignments which are so obvious to the ob-

e setting sun reappearing on the north side of the Ward Hill of Hoy from Maeshowe on 12th December

ALIGNMENTS

Midsummer sunset at the Standing Stones

During its monthly cycle, the Moon has a complex behaviour due to the nature of its orbit around the Earth. This renders it useless for celestial navigation, but adds great interest to the night sky. Lunar declination can change by up to 57° during any month.

The result is a considerable bonus for photographers as moonrise and moonset change in time and azimuth every day. An emphemeris is a very handy way to determine the movements of celestial bodies in advance. The website ephemeris.com is one good source of this data. The program The Photographer's Ephemeris is especially useful for planning photography shoots and is available from photoephemeris.com.

Megalithic Geometry Surveys of many of the 1,300 or so stone circles and settings in Britain have revealed that most were accurately laid out as circles, ellipses or flattened ellipses. Ropes and pegs would have been sufficient in many cases, but some form of measurement was essential to mark out where stones were to be erected and ditches to be dug.

server today are intended, but not with a high degree of geometrical accuracy.

This early "calendar" may well have been dependent on the lunar rather than the solar cycle. The growing seasons, tides and lunations were perhaps of greater importance than the more obvious movements of the sun. There are implications here for an as yet putative, but undiscovered, Neolithic calendar

The Moon was also clearly important in the Neolithic, as now. Predicting the tides would have been essential, but these people also knew about the more long term movements of the Moon, which are generally not understood by today's urban dwellers.

Alexander Thom and others have postulated *"Megalithic Feet, Yards, Rods"* and so on which in many cases seem to fit the actual measurements on the ground. Knowledge of triangles, especially the 3,4,5 would have been very helpful in laying out circles, cairns and houses.

Midsummer sunrise at Barnhouse

It is hard to imagine how a structure like Maeshowe could be designed without using units and angles. The recent excavations at the Ness of Brodgar further emphasise the planning, architectural and building abilities of the Neolithic people. Detailed engineering surveys will doubtless reveal much in future.

Sunrises and Sunsets The area around the Ring of Brodgar is especially atmospheric in every season and every time of day. The visitor can only speculate and wonder at the exceptional setting, perhaps for a time forgetting the modern world.

Although rarely mentioned in books and articles, the Ring of Bookan, just to the north of Brodgar, is another fascinating site. It has panoramic views of the West Mainland. All of the solar and lunar phenomena can be observed from here, where the slight elevation of 30m gives a clear view of the whole surroundings.

Sunset from Bookan Ring in early November

NEOLITHIC ART

Pierowall chambered cairn lintel stone

NEOLITHIC ART Until recently the subject of Neolithic Art in Orkney was not taken very seriously. Certainly there were chevron and lozenge incisions at Skara Brae and elsewhere. Cup marks, eyebrow motifs and whorls similar to those from other areas were also found, as were many exquisite carved stone and bone objects.

The range of artifacts which are found depends on the environment in which they have been since deposition. Apart

The Westray Wife

from bone, very few organic items have been discovered. This means that almost nothing is known about Neolithic wooden tools and fittings, boats, textiles, clothing or furnishings.

There is no evidence that these people used any kind of writing or notation. Equally their language is unknown. There are clear similarities with designs used in Ireland and southern England on pottery and on carved stones. Objects made from stone and jet which originated hundreds of miles away confirm trading links.

Skara Brae yielded a huge number of carved stone objects, jewellery made from bone and teeth, as well as symbols carved on stones. Many artifacts were carved from bone, ivory and whale's teeth. Perhaps the most impressive are two whale-bone pins which are 25cm long.

Westray The Links of Noltland is a large area of sand dunes above Grobust on Westray which is constantly changing.

Recent excavations there have revealed a Neolithic settlement. In 2009 the "Westray Wife" (or Orkney Venus) was found. This 3cm female figurine is by far the oldest carving of a person so far found in Scotland.

Two additional interesting objects were found here. In 2010 a second figurine was found, this time in clay and about 34mm high, though without its head. A much larger decorated stone 45cm high was also found here in 2008. It has incised chevrons and an S-shaped carving.

At Pierowall a carved stone was found during quarry work in 1981. It closely resembles a stone found on Eday. The carving is very similar to those at Newgrange in Ireland and was probably part of the lintel over the entrance of this Maeshowe-type tomb. The structure was destroyed before 2,000BC.

Tomb of the Eagles The first find at the chambered cairn at Isbister on South

Stone axe blade from the Knap of Howar

Ronaldsay was a cache of carved stone objects, including a mace head and small axe and knives. Carved bone and shell jewellery was found as well as a jet button and ring. The high quality workmanship can be admired at the site museum.

Knap of Howar The oldest standing stonebuilt house in Orkney was the site of some interesting finds, including a fine carved stone axe blade and a huge variety of bone and stone tools. Many of these are beautifully made and are more than merely utilitarian. The construction of the buildings is also very skilled.

Mace head from the Tomb of the Eagles

Incised stone from near hut 10, Skara Brae

NEOLITHIC POTTERY & TOOLS

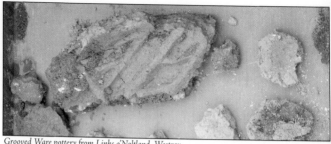

Grooved Ware pottery from Links o'Noltland, Westray

POTTERY was a major feature of the Neolithic Age in Orkney. It ranges from small bowls and drinking cups to containers capable of holding up to 100 litres. The pots are often beautifully made and decorated.

Both *Unstan* and *Grooved Ware* used decoration similar to other forms of Neolithic artwork. The former tend to be finer, round bottomed bowls and beakers, while the latter are more utilitarian and usually bucket shaped. The styles seem to be associated with particular sites.

Grooved Ware pottery sherds often make up a large fraction of the larger artifacts found during excavations. They frequently survive in remarkably good condition. Doubtless there were fashions in pots and perhaps rivalry between different potters.

A probable pottery kiln was discovered at the Knowes of Trotty but so far this is the only Neolithic example in Orkney. Potter Andrew Appleby has conducted some experiments with making and firing *Grooved Ware* type pottery.

"Grooved Ware" pottery sherd

"Unstan Ware" pottery from Isbister

Tomb of the Eagles jewelllery

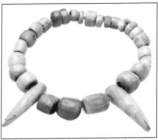
Bone jewellery from Skara Brae

Temperatures over 1,000°C were reached and a high yield of usable vessels resulted. Orkney clays need a high temperature to be properly fired. The kilns were built of turf and have used mixtures of peat, dung, wood and seaweed as fuel.

Jewellery artefacts have been found in large numbers, especially when bone survived well, as at Skara Brae and the Knap of Howar. Necklaces, bracelets and fine bone pins are most common. The latter were likely used to secure garments. Shells, whalebone, whales' teeth and Walrus ivory were also used.

Colouring Haematite was found at various sites. Some of the lumps were shiny, suggesting that they may have been used to polish leather. Some small pots contained red ochre, perhaps for personal adornment.

At Ness of Brodgar stones painted in red and yellow were found, suggesting that the use of colour may have been more widespread than previously thought. This raises many questions about the appearance of Neolithic buildings when they were in use.

Painted stone at the Ness of Brodgar

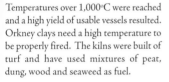

Neolithic haematite container

THE HEART OF NEOLITHIC ORKNEY

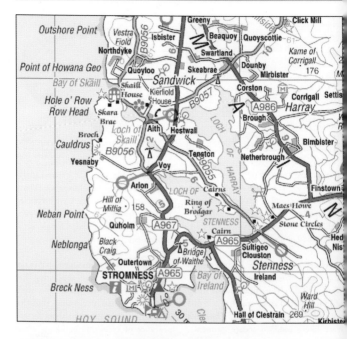

VISITING THE MONUMENTS

The spectacular Neolithic monuments of Orkney's West Mainland comprise of the UNESCO inscribed sites and a large number of associated places to visit. The recent discoveries at the Ness of Brodgar attest to what remains unknown about this remarkable period of prehistory.

Access Skara Brae and Maeshowe are open daily, with shorter hours in winter. All of the other sites are freely open,

apart from the Ness of Brodgar. This can only be seen while excavation work is in progress during July and August.

Most of the monuments are within a relatively compact area and are best appreciated by walking or cycling between them. Most have convenient car parking and public access by signed paths. Some of the isolated standing stones are best viewed from the road as they are in fields with no easy access.

NEOLITHIC MONUMENTS OF THE WEST MAINLAND

Skara Brae	p32	opening hours, admission charge, visitor centre, shop, cafeteria
Ring of Brodgar	p40	open at all times
Ness of Brodgar	p44	visits during excavation season, July and August
The Standing Stones	p48	open at all times
Watchstone	p50	open at all times
Maeshowe	p52	opening hours, admission charge, visitor centre, shop, bookable guided tours
Barnhouse Village	p62	open at all times
Barnhouse Stone	p62	open at all times
Unstan Cairn	p62	open at all times
Ring of Bookan	p63	open at all times
Deepdale Stone	p63	open at all times

Note: Only sites described in this book are listed here. For full information on Orkney's archaeological heritage please refer to *The Orkney Guide Book, 4th edition*

It should be noted that Maeshowe operates a system of tours, which must be booked in advance at busy periods (Tel 01856 761606). Skara Brae should be avoided when large cruise liners are visiting as it can get crowded at times. On such days it is best to visit early or late in the day (Tel 01856 841815).

Tours A number of operators run visits to the ancient sites. The major companies include Stagecoach and John o'-Groats Ferries which have tours in the summer. A number of smaller businesses operate all year. Current details are available from VisitOrkney Information Centres in Kirkwall and Stromness (Tel 01856 872856).

When to Visit? The best times to visit are frequently around sunrise and sunset, rather than in the middle of the day. Not only does this avoid the crowds, but offers by far the best lighting. Maeshowe is famous for its midwinter sunset, but this can be seen on any clear day between late November and late January.

All of the standing stones are at their most dramatic early and late in the day, which is when solar or lunar alignments may be best observed. Many of the monuments are also in line of sight of each other and this is more obvious at such times. Visiting out of the main tourist season allows for a much more tranquil and satisfying experience.

Skara Brae

Aerial view of Skara Brae

SKARA BRAE (HY232188), by the south shore of the Bay of Skaill, is unique. This remarkably well preserved Neolithic village is one of very few archeological sites where it is actually possible to imagine the life of the inhabitants.

Discovery It is said to have been first revealed after a severe northwesterly storm and extremely high tide in 1850. In fact

"the square catacombs in the Downs of Skaill" were commented on by James Robertson, who visited in the 1760s. Recent work has shown that this prehistoric community was occupied for at least 600 years, from before 3200BC to about 2500BC. There is evidence of earlier layers dating from 3500BC, while secondary usage continued until about 2200BC.

Professor V Gordon Childe with visitors

Hut 1 before being tidied up

Excavation Four houses were cleared out in the 1860s, but no further work was done until the site was taken into state care in 1925. In the meantime, further storms washed away most of hut 3 and part of hut 1. A sea wall was built to protect the site from further damage. Professor V Gordon Childe was brought in to supervise its recording and conservation in 1929.

The complexity of the ruins and the need to preserve the structures made a proper stratigraphic excavation impossible, but clear evidence of several phases of occupation were revealed. This also means that a great deal remains for future investigators to reveal.

Skerrabrae The name Skara Brae is a recent 20th century corruption of *Skerrabra*, as it is still known as locally, the *brae* part being a mapmaker's corruption. It is perhaps from ON *Skjaldbreiðr*, Broad Shield, as the former mound resembled a Norse shield. Alternatively the name may come from ON *Skerabreiðr*, Broad Skerry, referring to the large area of rocks which protects the site from the west. In former times the settlement was probably separated from the sea by sand dunes and dune slacks, which have since been eroded away.

Village Having been cocooned within a large dune for over 4,500 years, the village is remarkably preserved. The group of seven houses is connected by a covered close, all of which were buried to the tops of the walls by midden. This clay-like mixture of refuse consists of ashes, shells, bones, sand and other domestic detritus, which has been a major factor in protecting the site from erosion.

It seems that the occupants built the midden around their houses intentionally as an integral part of the construction. The material appears to have been stored and used deliberately rather than simply piled round existing houses. The earlier dwellings appear to have been free standing like those at Barnhouse.

Houses The huts vary in size from over 6m square to barely 4m square, with a

Rough seas break over Skara Brae

Hut 7 is now hidden by a turfed over roof and is the lowest, and presumably oldest, level

maximum surviving wall height of 2.4m. The designs are quite similar with beds, dressers, tanks in the floor, cupboards in the walls and cells off the main room. A system of stone lined drains, which connect to several of the side cells, serves the village, to remove rainwater, and no doubt domestic waste. Childe describes green slime being found in the drains, but none was kept for analysis.

Each house has a central fireplace and a doorway exiting to the main passage. These were small, about 1.1m high by 0.6m wide, and very carefully constructed. There was provision to fasten the doors from the inside. The dressers are prominently placed facing the entrance. In the later houses, stone box beds stand beside the sidewalls.

Aerial view of Skara Brae

Stone saddle quern

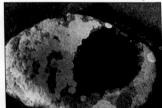

Hut 8 is on the left, seen from the south swith the kiln and street on the right

The interiors are surprisingly spacious with a floor area of up to 36m². Damp proof courses had also been invented over 5,000 years ago. The foundations of the houses have a layer of blue clay in the bottom course, which would have worked as well as polythene does today.

The earliest houses resemble those at Barnhouse, with beds recessed in the walls, while the later ones are larger with freestanding boxbeds. During the 600 years or more of primary occupation the buildings were repaired, modified and re-built, apart from hut 7, which is built on a clay base directly on the sand.

Two older women were buried under one wall, perhaps before the house was built. It has been suggested that this was a

Stone dresser in hut 1

The Street joins the houses underground

Hut 8 is different and was probably the workshop, kiln and barn

foundation burial and that the hut had a different use to the others. Although no drains have been found leading from hut 7, two of the compartments had thick layers of green sludge.

What remains today is like a fossil. There would have been driftwood from America available for furnishings and materials such as animal sheepskins, leather and eider down, as well as caisies, cubbies and the original Orkney chairs.

The north entrance to hut 8

There is no evidence for fabrics and no remains of anything to do with weaving. No spindles or whorls were found. However fibres from Nettle stems were probably used to make fishing lines and nets, and perhaps clothes. Heather stems would have provided ropes and wool was undoubtedly used to make cloth, perhaps by felting rather than weaving.

The roofs must have been supported by couples made of driftwood or whale-bones and covered with skins or turf, held down by flat stones, heather ropes and straw simmons. There was probably a hole to let out the smoke and to admit some light. House 7 has spaces in the top courses, which look like they are for the fitting of joists.

The street and doorways are narrow, so there may easily have been roof entrances to facilitate the moving of large objects like pots. Most likely these roomy houses had internal galleries for storage and sleeping. There is no direct evidence for this but a visit to the replica house makes this obvious.

The Workshop One building, hut 8, was apparently the workshop, as it has no beds and is differently arranged. It is to the south of the houses and was not surrounded by midden. Many fragments of chert, which had been heated, were found on the floor. In the absence of flint this stone was used to make cutting and scraping tools.

There was a kiln probably for firing pottery, and drying grain and malt. Large pots were made in sizes up to 60cm diameter, which were often decorated with geometric patterns. This is classed as *Grooved Ware*, which was also found at Barnhouse, the Standing Stones, Rinyo and in some of the Maeshowe-type chambered cairns.

The porch on the east end has opposing doors and has been interpreted as an area for winnowing of corn, while the building was probably also a grain storage and processing area, and may have been used to malt barley. The large pots could hold at least 100 litres and would have been used for storage, but may well also have functioned as containers for making ale. Apart from this usage, malted barley is very digestible, and much more palatable

Hut 5 has beds built into the walls and is older

to people and ruminants than the grain. Once dried, malt stores very well.

Lifestyle The inhabitants kept cattle, pigs and sheep. They grew barley and some wheat, fished the nearby waters, caught birds and gathered shellfish. Bone was much used for tools and jewellery. The soil conditions were not favourable for the preservation of wood and thus very little has survived. In 1972 a waterlogged area was investigated and yielded a heather rope and a wooden handle. Most such artefacts have not survived, but it must be assumed that the Skara Brae people used many wooden objects.

Hut 4 is one of the older, smaller houses

Skara Brae

Replica of hut 8 at the Visitor Centre

There would have been plenty of driftwood from North America, which would have been used for multiple purposes. The villagers must have had reasonably good boats to go fishing, with wooden and with leather or woven covering, sown and strengthened with nettle fibre.

Artefacts Many artefacts were discovered including numerous circular stone pot lids, bone tools and jewellery. Four carved stone objects were also found, similar to others found in Orkney and elsewhere in Scotland. It has always been assumed that these special objects had some significant purpose associated with ritual and that somehow the inhabitants were totally different to people today.

Neolithic Art also appears in the many motifs which have been scratched on stones at Skara Brae, especially in huts 7 and 8 and in the street near hut 2. They may be seen by visitors on the east side of hut 8 and at the south entrance to the street. Made up of lozenges, chevrons, crosses and triangles, these motifs resemble those on *Grooved Ware* pots and similar inscriptions from Brodgar and Barnhouse as well as Maeshowe, Quoyness, Cuween and Wideford Hill cairns.

Skaill knives were common, and are made by chipping shards off beach stones to give a useful sharp edge. One of these is decorated with the patterns already described. There is a pervasive feeling that

Carved stone bulls horns with incised marks

Carved geometric stone object

"Grooved Ware" pottery

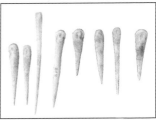

Bone pins

these shapes and symbols have meanings, but if they do they remain elusive. No organic artefacts have survived with these symbols.

Evidence has not been found of any material objects from outside Orkney, suggesting a self-sufficient lifestyle. That contacts with communities from further afield occurred is clear from the pottery and artwork. Boats good enough to fish off to the west of Orkney are certainly adequate to cross the Pentland Firth and traverse the coast of Britain.

Abandonment of the settlement around 2500BC was very likely caused by encroaching sand, perhaps slowly as the dunes shifted and the surrounding land became inundated. A great storm could have caused the village to be overwhelmed. However some of the houses continued in use for at least another 300 years, as shown by the multiple occupation layers in the sand which filled them.

The Visitor Centre has an introductory video about Skara Brae and the Neolithic Age in Orkney. Hands on interpretative displays, plus a range of artefacts and diagrams give a good perspective on the site. The impressive replica of hut 7 gives a dramatic idea of just how cosy and spacious they were. There is also a café and a well stocked shop.

Whalebone carved pendants

"Grooved Ware" pottery designs

THE RING OF BRODGAR

September evening light at the Ring of Brodgar

THE RING OF BRODGAR (ON *Bruar-gardr*, Bridge Farm) is one of the finest stone circles anywhere. This great henge monument is superbly situated on the Ness of Brodgar, in a confluence of water and sky, surrounded by the agricultural heart of Orkney. The feeling of spaciousness is enhanced by the size of the circle, which is 103.7m in diameter. Of the probable original 60 stones, 27 remain standing, varying between 2.1m and 4.7m in height. The site is laid out very accurately in a perfect circle, with the stones approximately 6 degrees apart.

The source of the stones has been the subject of speculation but the most likely quarry is in Sandwick, near Vestrafiold, where prepared megaliths can still be seen. The sandstone beds here are of good quality and were clearly suitable for making standing stones. Two unused examples lie on the shore of the Loch of Stenness near Wasbister Barrow, suggesting that they may perhaps have been transported by water for part of the way.

The surrounding rock cut ditch is now 10m across but it was originally 5m wide and more than 3m deep. It is now half silted up and the sides have eroded. Radiocarbon dating of this infill places the digging of the ditch in the third millennium BC.

Despite the volume of material dug out, there is no trace of a surrounding earthwork, although there may originally have been a bank. An estimated 4,700m³ of rock shifted to complete the excavation. There are two entrance causeways, on the northwest and southeast sides.

Comet Stone About 140m to the southeast an isolated menhir, the Comet Stone (ON *Kuml-stein*, Mound Stone), is set on a platform beside the stumps of two other stones. At spring and autumn equinoxes, viewed from here, the sun sets just glancing off the westernmost side of the Ring of Brodgar. Several other stones stand between this and the Bridge of Brodgar. There are also at least eight large mounds and smaller tumuli in the area, which are probably Bronze Age. It seems that the Brodgar area remained important during the 3rd and 2nd millennia BC at least, and today it still has a magnetic attraction.

Alignments There are a variety of astronomical alignments, which may have been intended by the builders. While many stones are missing, simple observation suggests several possibilities. These relate to the solstices and the equinoxes as well as times such as *Beltane* (Old May Day). At winter and summer solstices the sunrises and sunsets align with stones and notches in the hills. Other outlying standing stones may be markers for specific times of year also.

Winter sunrise at the Ring of Brodgar

The site was undoubtedly chosen for observation of the moon. During major lunar standstills, every 18.6 years, the moon appears to skim the Orphir hills as seen from Brodgar. The phenomenon was visible several times during 2005 to 2007. Every lunar month the moon passes low over the southern horizon when at its lowest declination.

Geophysical scans of the area showed evidence of settlement to the south on the Ness of Brodgar, and to the north in the Wasbister area. A Bronze Age figure-of-eight house lies under one small mound, and it is probable that more Neolithic and later sites will also be found.

The Ring of Brodgar

Midsummer sunset at the Ring of Brodgar from the Comet Stone

Perhaps the most interesting finding is that there is no evidence of any buildings in the vicinity of the Ring of Brodgar itself.

Dyke o'Sean The Dyke o'Sean is an ancient turf embankment which crosses the Ness of Brodgar north of the ring, and is the traditional parish boundary between Sandwick and Stenness. There are also references to a similar dyke to the south,

suggesting that the area around the Ring of Brodgar was in some way special and demarcated from the land outside the dykes. This is consistent with the lack of finds within the ring itself, suggesting that this area was in some way special.

The Ring of Brodgar was taken into state guardianship in 1906 and several fallen stones were re-erected. Lightning strikes have since shattered two. There is very

The Ring of Brodgar on a summer evening

Midsummer sunrise at the Ring of Brodgar

little graffiti to deface the monoliths, but one stone on the North side is inscribed by some cryptographic Norse tree runes, thought to stand for *Bjorn*. The inscription was found on the lower side of a fallen stone when it was re-erected in 1907, and may well be genuine.

The variety of lighting conditions at different seasons and hours, for which Orkney is justly famous, is nowhere more evident than at this ancient site. The builders certainly knew what they were doing when they chose this position at the centre of the West Mainland. There are few more evocative places to be at dawn or sunset at any time of year than the Ring of Brodgar, a precinct to enjoy and perhaps where one can temporarily escape from time itself. It really is a special place to visit whatever the season, time of day or weather.

Midwinter sunset from the Ring of Brodgar

THE NESS OF BRODGAR

Ness of Brodgar under excavation

NESS OF BRODGAR is the narrow peninsula north of the bridge from which the area takes its name. There must have been a crossing here since the earliest times. In 1925 a stone decorated with Neolithic lozenges and chevrons was found in the area now being excavated. It had been reused as the lid of a Bronze Age cist burial. This was sent to the National Museum and quietly forgotten.

Luckily the field was never subjected to deep ploughing as at Barnhouse.

Discovery Geophysical surveys in the Brodgar area in 2003 showed many possible structures "indicative of settlement". Exploratory trenches were dug in 2004, which revealed the presence of a large area of Neolithic structures. Over the last few years several large buildings have

"Brodgar Boy" figurine

Side cell built into wall

been revealed. They have a strong similarity to the main building at nearby Barnhouse.

Walls The site is bounded to the north and south by well built walls. The northern one was initially 4m wide, later widened to 6m, and up to 100m long. The southern one is 2m across, but survives to a height of 1.7m. They were paved on the outside and must have been most impressive. They could have been 3m or more high and enclose an area roughly 125m by 75m. They divide the recently excavated structures from the rest of the landscape. The oldest radiocarbon dates found so far are from material under the southern wall and are from c.3200BC.

Buildings The largest building, structure 10, is 20m square with walls 5m thick. It is surrounded by paving and has stonework of remarkable quality. The cross shaped interior includes standing stones and in design is reminiscent of Maeshowe, with which the entrance seems to be aligned.

Brodgar Stone found in 1925

All of these buildings have side chambers built into the walls, central fireplaces and are aligned roughly north to south. Large quantities of *Grooved Ware* pottery as well as polished mace heads, carved and incised stones, a carved whale's tooth and stones with peck marks have been found. In 2011 the "Brodgar Boy" clay figurine added to the growing finds of anthropomorphic artefacts in Orkney.

Paving stones and high quality walling

Walling found in 2008

THE NESS OF BRODGAR

Aerial view of the Ness of Brodgar; the excavation site is the field in the right foreground

Painted Stones One of the most interesting finds was painted stones. Probably iron based pigments mixed with animal fat or egg whites were used to create the yellow, red and brown coatings. Some have scratched designs which would have been very obvious when new and which resemble other incised Neolithic artwork. Haematite and "paint pots" have been found at many Orkney Neolithic sites, and it was formerly assumed that these were for personal adornment. It now appears that paint was used to decorate at least parts of these buildings.

Flagstone Roofs Evidence was found suggesting that these buildings were at least partly roofed by flagstone slates in

the same manner as traditional Orkney houses. A layer of large, worked rectangular flagstones was discovered on the floor of two of the structures. The rectangular "slates" had been skillfully trimmed. So far no evidence has been found of post holes, suggesting that the roofs must have been free standing. Perhaps these buildings would not have looked so unfamiliar to modern Orcadians.

Interiors Dressers and central hearths similar to those at Skara Brae were present, but the scale of the buildings and lack of evidence for long term occupation suggests that these were not houses for living in. More probably they were used

46

for special occasions as has previously been suggested for Barnhouse. There is a general lack of household rubbish and so far no small buildings such as those at Skara Brae or the Knap of Howar have been discovered.

Despite its massive size, the inside of structure 10 is only slightly larger than Maeshowe at about 6m across. The surviving interior stone work is however not of the standard of its neighbour, but this may reflect demolition and robbing rather than the original workmanship.

Alignments The entrance of structure 10 faces over the Loch of Stenness to Barnhouse, the Standing Stones of Stenness, and perhaps most importantly, to Maeshowe. It faces in a southeasterly direction, towards the midwinter sunrise, which from here appears over Mid Hill in Orphir. There are obviously many other possibilities for other solar or lunar alignments from the Ness of Brodgar. Some of these may become evident as excavation continues.

Abandonment The latest radiocarbon dates so far found are c.2300BC from cattle bones around structure 10. This was first built around 2600BC and involved much demolition and burial of earlier buildings. Development continued for about 300 years, after which structure 10 was put out of use. It was filled with midden and rubble.

Hundreds of cattle tibia were also found here, perhaps representing feasting at the final closure of the site. Neolithic activity continued for perhaps another 200 years, but on a minor scale.

Nick Card, Project Manager has said, *"The discoveries are unparalleled in British prehistory, the complexity of finds is changing the whole vision of what the landscape was 5,000 years ago and that it's of a scale that almost relates to the classical period in the Mediterranean with walled enclosures and walled precincts. The site could be more important than Stonehenge."*

Inscribed stone

Broken carved stone mace head

STANDING STONES OF STENNESS

The Standing Stones in the late 18ᵗʰ century with the Odin Stone on the right

STANDING STONES OF STENNESS
This stone circle originally had up to 12 monoliths and a diameter of 30m, but now comprises of only 4 uprights, the tallest of which is over 5m high. It is surrounded by a rock cut ditch 2m deep, 7m wide and 44m in diameter which has become filled in over the years. Excavation revealed a square setting of stones and holes for further uprights, either stone or wooden.

Midsummer sunset

Remains of domestic animals, including cattle, sheep and dog bones as well as a human finger were found in the ditch. Sherds of *Grooved Ware* pottery were also present. Radiocarbon dating indicates that the circle was built about 3100BC, which is older than many henge monuments further south in Britain. It is probably contemporary with Barnhouse Village and the older parts of the Ness of Brodgar.

There are several possible lunar and solar alignments visible from here. In midsummer the sun rises over a notch in the Ren-

Midwinter sunrise over the Standing Stones of Stenness at about 09:50GMT

dall hills and sets far to the north over the Sandwick hills, while in midwinter it rises over the Orphir Hills and sets over Hoy. During major lunar standstills (every 18.6 years) the moon skims the Orphir hills, and it seems likely that observation of this event may have been part of the Neolithic ritual.

In midwinter the moon rises over Maeshowe at sunset. There is an interesting alignment from the Standing Stones with Maeshowe, which appears centred between the two prominent uprights to the north of the central hearth. This may be fortuitous as so much of the monument is no longer standing.

The sun "flashing" on the north flank of the Ward Hill of Hoy on 11th December

STANDING STONES OF STENNESS

Watchstone sunset on 8ᵗʰ January over the Hoy Hills and the Loch of Stenness

Springtime at the Watchstone

Watchstone At the Bridge of Brodgar, stands the Watchstone (HY305128, 5.6m). From it the date of the winter solstice may be determined on at least four different days. About ten days before and after midwinter the sun reappears momentarily in a notch on the north side of the Ward Hill of Hoy, after setting behind its southern flank.

Another interesting alignment from the Watchstone occurs on Up Helli Day, twelve days after Old New Year, still celebrated in Shetland with Up Helly Aa. On this date, around the 29ᵗʰ of January, the sun disappears behind Cuilags just before sunset and then reappears for a moment below the Kame of Hoy, before finally setting. This also happens on about the 11th of November.

The Watchstone, on the left, with the Odin Stone, on the right, before destruction

Odinstone This stone was destroyed in 1814 and used as lintels by the tenant farmer at Barnhouse, a ferrylouper who had become irritated by visitors to the stones. Apparently the part with the hole was used as the pivot for a horse mill but was destroyed after WWII.

Luckily the selfish farmer was stopped from demolishing the rest of the Standing Stones, but only after he had toppled two more of the menhirs, one of which he broke up. The threat of Court action finally stopped this 19th century vandal, and the fallen stone was re-erected in 1906.

Luckily the vast majority of landowners over the millennia have had great respect for our antiquities.

The Odinstone had a hole in it through which lovers clasped hands and swore their everlasting troth. The Oath of Odin was then said and the contract was binding thereafter. The Stone was also credited with healing powers, in association with the well at Bigswell (HY345105), especially at *Beltane* and midsummer. Recently the probable sockets of both this stone and another were found between the Standing Stones and the Watch Stone.

Reappearing sun at the Kame of Hoy on 29th January

MAESHOWE

The interior of Maeshowe showing two cells, blocking stones and the entrance passage with buttresses

MAESHOWE (HY315128), considered to be one of the greatest architectural achievements of Neolithic Europe, is Orkney's largest and finest chambered cairn. The *Orkneyinga Saga* refers to it as *Orkahaugr* (ON The Mound of the Orks).

Another derivation may be ON *Mathhaugr*, meadow mound. There is a Maesquoy about 5km (3mi) north of Maeshowe on the Netherbrough Road. There are also several farm names which end in "may", so this could well be the correct meaning, if rather mundane.

The mound, 35m in diameter and 7m high, consists mostly of packed stones and clay, with an inner layer of masonry around the chamber. A stone and concrete roof was installed after it was cleared out in

1861. Before this it was rather higher in profile. Other unrecorded repairs to the outer end of the entrance passage were also made, which means that the original entrance layout is unknown.

Maeshowe was included in the first Ancient Monuments Act of 1882, and has been in state care since 1910. It was designed and constructed with great attention to detail, the large dressed slabs being skillfully set together and finished by master stonemasons. The chamber is 4.5m square and about the same in height. A tapered orthostat faces each corner buttress giving an impression of space and strength. The original roof design and height is unknown, but it may have been 6m high.

There are three cells within the walls which were sealed with stone blocks now on the floor. The entrance passage, 14.5m long and 1.4m high, is lined with huge slabs, the largest weighing over 30 tonnes. When opened in 1861, the building was empty bar a piece of human skull, and some horse bones, but this was certainly not the first such incursion. The Vikings visited during the 12th century and left one of the largest collections of runes anywhere.

Maeshowe was built on a levelled area of ground with a surrounding bank and ditch, peat from the bottom of which has been dated at 2750BC, which makes it contemporary with the Standing Stones and Skara Brae. Since no artefacts were found in 1861, little can be deduced about its usage. The surrounding bank was rebuilt on top of an original drystone wall in early Norse times.

Evidence of sockets for large standing stones around the outside of the mound only adds mystery to the original design and purpose. Carvings on some of the stones very similar to those found at Skara

Aerial view of Maeshowe in the snow

Brae and the Ness of Brodgar, are present. The overriding impression is of a Neolithic Cathedral, not a simple tomb.

While the other Maeshowe-type chambered cairns are all very well constructed, only Maeshowe itself is truly monumental, with huge slabs of stone. Each cell is roofed by a single massive flagstone weighing up to 30 tonnes. After 5,000 years there has been little settlement and only a few of the horizontal slabs have cracked, attesting to the competence of the engineers who built the cairn.

Maeshowe is surrounded by a circular ditch and bank

MAESHOWE - WINTER SUNSET

Midwinter sunset illuminating the passage and floor

Winter solstice It has long been known that the setting sun shines directly down the passage of Maeshowe around the winter solstice, lighting up the back wall and passage in a dramatic fashion. Much speculation has been published over the years about this.

The large blocking stone at the entrance seems designed to be shut from the inside, but also would leave a gap of about 20cm to allow light through. The floor of the passage slopes up towards the chamber, so that water runs outwards towards a drain. Some collects at the entrance and acts as a reflector, greatly increasing the illumination of the interior when the sun is bright.

From mid-November until mid-January the sun shines into the chamber at sunset and lights up the back wall, gradually creeping down the passage and across the floor. At the winter solstice the shaft of light hits the back wall at about 14:40GMT, and by 15:05 the sun has set behind the Ward Hill of Hoy.

As the shortest day approaches, the sun sets further south until eventually it disappears behind the Ward Hill of Hoy. For several days it reappears some minutes later on the north side of the hill, sending a beam of light down the east side of the passage and lighting up a patch on the back wall. About 20 days before the solstice the sun briefly flashes before setting, but for the next 40 days it does not reappear in this fashion, as it is too low in the sky.

A similar alignment can be observed about 40 days before and after the winter solstice, when the setting sun disappears behind the Cuilags on Hoy and then briefly reappears below the Kame. Thus there are at least five days when observations can determine the actual shortest day.

Maeshowe was most carefully placed in its environment. Today it is impossible to devine the original layout, since many

About three weeks before and after the solstice

standing stones and other features have been destroyed, and thus further alignments may well have existed. What is clear is that the builders had a definite vision and purpose. Ceremonies were undoubtedly held here, which would have included those for the dead, but also for the living and perhaps the return of the sun.

The sun hitting the back wall

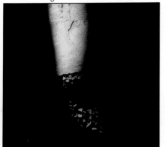

12th January sun on blocking stone

Maeshowe - Runes

No9 "Ingibjorg, the fair widow. Many a woman has gone stooping in here. A great show-off."

RUNES Maeshowe has one of the largest groups of Norse runic inscriptions known. They are common all over Scandinavia and the Norse colonies, with the earliest dating from about 200AD. The younger *fuzark* was developed about 700AD and was the form of runes used by the Vikings. Many inscriptions are on artefacts and tell who carved the runes. Runic memorial stones are common, often using existing boulders to commemorate the exploits of the dead.

Few such inscriptions have been found in Orkney, possibly because of the nature of the sandstone. Fragments only remain of what must have been a larger number. Graffiti writing has presumably been a popular pastime for many years, but is usually regarded as a mess to be cleared up, rather than something to marvel at.

Runes developed as a way of carving letters into wood, bone or stone using a blade or

No32 "...treasure was hidden here";"Happy is he who can find the great wealth.........."

similar implement. They represent most of the Latin alphabet, as required by Old Norse. There are many variations in the runic alphabet, but most of the characters have Latin equivalents. Runes were used throughout the Germanic lands, but were probably developed in Scandinavia.

The Maeshowe runes were carved in the 12th century, some by returning crusaders. There are about 30 inscriptions, many of the style, *"Thorfinn wrote these runes"*. Some gave the father's name, or a nickname, others are by women and several are about them.

Clearly the Vikings were interested in Maeshowe and left inscriptions on at least one other occasion, when stories about treasure were being told, as in *"Haakon singlehanded bore treasures from this howe"*. The very long inscription on the monolith to the northwest of the entrance passage describes how *"Treasure was carried away three nights before they broke this mound."* In other words a lame excuse for the Vikings not finding any of what they would call treasure.

Women were also discussed, as in No9, *"Ingibjorg the fair widow"*. *"Many a woman has come stooping in here. A great showoff. Erlingr"*. No10 is less polite, *"Þorny fucked. Helgi carved."* Or No5, quite mundane, *"Vermundr carved."*

Gaukr's Axe No20 is on two separate blocks on the southeast side of the chamber. *"The man who is most skilled in runes west of the ocean carved these runes with the axe which*

"No4 That will be true which I say, that treasure was carried away. Treasure was carried away three nights before they broke this mound."

MAESHOWE - RUNES

"No20 The man who is most skilled in runes west of the ocean carved these runes with the axe...

Gaukr Trandilssonr owned south of the country [Iceland]".

The carver may have been Thorhallr Asgrimssom, according to the *Orkneyinga Saga*, captain of Earl Rognvald's ship when they returned in 1153 from the Crusades. He was the great great grandson of Asgrimr Ellidtha-Grimssonr, who is claimed to have killed Gaukr Trandilson in the late 900s in

A coiled serpent, perhaps a "Krakken"

Iceland. If true the axe must have remained in this family for 5 generations.

Tree Runes Some, including no20, have cryptic tree runes which are easily deciphered by a numeric code based on the *fuzark*, the runic alphabet. Little could the Viking graffiti writers of c.1152 have realised how interesting their runes would be today! In the magnificent setting of Maeshowe, the Viking visitors seem not so far away.

Simple graffiti No1 is typical of many of the inscriptions. High on the southwest wall above the entrance passage is a very clear inscription which read, *"That is a Viking...then came underneath to this place".*

Maeshowe Dragon The Maeshowe Dragon is a very familiar Orkney icon, which has been interpreted in various ways. Most Orcadians consider that it is a mythical dragon. Some try to interpret it as a motif depicting pagan beliefs being killed by a Christian sword.

This seems unlikely since the Vikings had been converted for over 150 years. Others think it is a lion. Rognvald and his men had just been to Jerusalem and the crusades, visiting Venice along the way, which could have inspired a dragon or a lion. Whatever the thoughts of the artist, it looks fresh after over 860 years.

Below the dragon there is an animal which is probably a Common Seal, which would fit very well with the Norse name for Maeshowe. The fanciful have suggested that it may be an Otter or even a Walrus. Again there is common local agreement that it is indeed a selkie.

Further down an intricately knotted sea serpent, perhaps a *kraaken* appears almost to writhe. This worm-knot is of a similar stan-

The "Maeshowe Dragon"

dard to the dragon. Visitors must make up their own minds as to what these carvings may be intended to represent, but none can deny the craftsmanship and beauty of these 12th century graffiti. Today we strongly discourage such things, but at the same time these Norsemen immeasurably increased the interest of a visit to Maeshowe.

No1 "That is a viking...then came underneath to this place"

Unstan has stalls and a side chamber

Unstan Cairn (HY283118), near the Brig o'Waithe has given its name to a class of Neolithic pottery, *Unstan Ware*. When excavated in 1884, a large amount of this was found. These bowls have a characteristic shape and decoration and were also found at the Knap of Howar on Papay, as well as in other stalled cairns of this type, including the Tomb of the Eagles in South Ronaldsay, which are referred to as the Orkney-Cromarty group.

Unstan interior from the south end

The chamber is 6.6m long, 1.9m at its widest and the walls survive to over 2m in height. Opening onto the side of the chamber, the narrow passage is 6.5m long. There is a cell in the centre of the wall opposite the entrance, and vertical flagstone stalls divide the main chamber into five sections, three central and two shelved end compartments which have end walls formed from large slabs set on edge. The whole design is very similar to the Tomb of the Eagles.

A stone with carvings and runes was put there during restoration, and while the runes may be Viking, the other shapes are more likely 20th century graffiti. A large amount of human and animal bone was found but unfortunately it was not recorded. Of particular interest is the northeast alignment of the entry passage with the Watchstone and the large house at Barnhouse Village across the loch. Towards midsummer the rising sun illuminates this passage.

Unstan Cairn may possibly date from as early as 3200BC. When it was cleared out in 1884 very little of the large assemblage of human and animal bones was kept. No samples of the "black layer" from the floor of the side cell were kept.

Barnhouse Stone This monolith (HY312122, 3.2m) stands in a field near the main road, inside a rather mean-looking fence put there by a farmer who would have preferred to have destroyed

One of the small houses at Barnhouse Village resembles the older ones at Skara Brae

it. It is positioned such that about 22 days before and after the winter solstice the setting sun lines up with this stone and the Maeshowe passage as it "flashes" on the north side of the Ward Hill of Hoy. The stone is also in alignment with the Watchstone and the centre of the Ring of Brodgar.

Barnhouse Village lies on the shore of the Loch of Harray about 100m from the Standing Stones. Despite deep ploughing, enough of the foundations remained to show a remarkable series of buildings. The small structures closely resemble the older houses at Skara Brae with central fireplaces, stone-lined drains and bed spaces set into the walls. The larger house has echoes of Maeshowe, but measures 7m square on the inside and has a large central hearth.

Grooved Ware pottery was found here and the oldest date seems to be about 3200BC, making it contemporary with the nearby Standing Stones. The houses may have been used for activities related to those at the stone circle. The small house nearest the loch and the entrance to the large house are aligned with mid-summer sunset. The entrance of one of the other houses is in line with the mid-winter sunrise.

Maeshowe 21st December from Barnhouse

Bookan & Deepdale

Sunset over Cuilags and Skae Frue from the centre of the Ring of Bookan on December 17ᵗʰ

Bookan To the north of Brodgar the Ring of Bookan (HY283145) is of particular interest. This henge monument has a ditch over 2m deep and 10m wide, which is partially filled-in. There is a central mound, about 42m by 38m, with a much-robbed chambered cairn at its centre, whose entrance faces the midsummer sunrise. Sweeping views over the Lochs of Harray and Stenness to the Hoy Hills and to Sandwick suggest that the site may have played an important part in the overall Neolithic plan.

To the southwest a substantial mound called Skae Frue is possibly a Bronze Age burial mound, but it also lies in a direct line with the midwinter sunset seen from the centre of the Ring of Bookan. This may well be another observation site for solar and lunar events.

Southeast lie a series of mounds and a substantial quarry of unknown date which was perhaps the source of stone for the nearby monuments and the buildings around Brodgar. Whether it was also a source for monoliths is unknown.

The entrance of the large ruined chambered cairn at the Ring of Bookan faces midsummer sunrise

The view towards Brodgar from Bookan chambered cairn

Bookan Cairn Facing the Ring of Brodgar, and about 400m southeast of the Ring of Bookan, little remains of Bookan chambered cairn (HY287141). It is unusual in that the interior divisions were vertically-placed flagstones set in a rectangular drystone building about 4m square. A short entrance passage leads to the main chamber, a central area about 2m by 1.3m, with five compartments, each about 1m square, two on each side and one at the far end.

Each compartment could be sealed off by means of an upright flagstone. In addition the cairn is surrounded by a stone wall, making the whole arrangement akin to Maeshowe-type tombs. Some pottery and bones were found and "lost" during the 1861 excavation. Bookan is different to most of the other chambered cairns in Orkney, but it does resemble Taversoe Tuick (Upper) on Rousay and Hunter-squoy (Upper) on Eday. There are also echoes of house interiors at Skara Brae and Knap of Howar.

Deepdale stones The large 2m-high monolith at Deepdale on the road to Stromness (HY272118) overlooks the Loch of Stenness and the Brig o' Waithe. Its flat side faces the Ring of Brodgar, and the stone may well have played a role in midsummer sunrise observations. It could also be related to nearby Unstan chambered cairn. Until recently there was another one nearby but it has disappeared. It remains popular today as a convenient rubbing post for cattle, and is worth visiting for the panoramic view of the centre of the West Mainland alone.

Deepdale standing stone

INDEX